Carrying On

Carrying On

Poems by

Mark Williams

© 2022 Mark Williams. All rights reserved.
This material may not be reproduced in any form, published,
reprinted, recorded, performed, broadcast,
rewritten or redistributed without
the explicit permission of Mark Williams.
All such actions are strictly prohibited by law.

Cover design by Shay Culligan
Cover photo by Timon Studler

ISBN: 978-1-63980-132-9

Kelsay Books
502 South 1040 East, A-119
American Fork, Utah 84003
Kelsaybooks.com

for DeeGee,
who keeps my wheel turning

Acknowledgments

Thanks to the editors of the following publications where these poems appeared:

The Southern Review: "Stridulation," "Fractals," "Carrying On"
The Lake: "In the Blue Box" and "King of Albania"
Rattle: "Identity Theft"
Open 24 Hours: "Mr. Know-It-All," "Speaking of Tongues," and "In a Bed of Purple Iris"
Landslide Lit (erary): "Voyagers"
The American Journal of Poetry: "Stripping Down to Fundamentalists," "Pep Talks, The Movie," "Blue Parakeets," and "My Forest Fire"
Nimrod: "Aspirations"
Typishly: "The Hokey Pokey"
New Ohio Review: "The New Yorker Cartoon Caption Contest"
Dodging the Rain: "Autobituary"
The Write Launch: "Fred's Theory of Relativity" and "Heaven's Rules"

"In the Blue Box" was included in the e-book anthology, *The Burden of Light, Poems on Illness and Loss* (Smashwords).

"Identity Theft" was included in the anthology *New Poetry from the Midwest 2014* (New American Press).

"Fractals" was included in the anthology *New Poetry from the Midwest 2017* (New American Press). It also appeared on the Indiana Humanities website.

"Carrying On" was included in the anthology, *The Sixty-Four: Best Poets of 2018* (The Black Mountain Press).

"Relax," by Ellen Bass, appears in her book, *Like a Beggar,* published by Copper Canyon Press in February 2014.

Special thanks to Linda Neal Reising, who made my poems better.

Thanks also to DeeGee Williams, Teresa Roy, Alison Baumann, Jessica Thompson, Tom Raithel, Caroline Nellis, Barbara Bennett and Barbara Stahura for their friendship, help, and encouragement. And thank you, Timon Studler, for your brilliant cover photo.

Contents

1

Stridulation	13
In the Blue Box	15
King of Albania	18
Identity Theft	19
Mr. Know-It-All	27
Speaking of Tongues	30
Voyagers	33
In a Bed of Purple Iris	35

2

Fred's Theory of Relativity	39
Has Becky Wright Returned *A Prayer for Owen Meany?*	42
Stripping Down to Fundamentalists	47
Fractals	49
Aspirations	57
Pep Talks, The Movie	60

3

Blue Parakeets	69
The Hokey Pokey	73
The New Yorker Cartoon Caption Contest	75
My Forest Fire	82
Carrying On	85
Heaven's Rules	92
Autobituary	95

1

Stridulation

In the insect room at the Louisville Science Center,
waiting for the next IMAX presentation of *Dolphins,*
I learned that termites, with great cooperative skill
(and equal part saliva), build mounds the equivalent height
of three Empire State Buildings; that if we were an ant,
the beech leaf across our back would weigh 500 pounds,
plus the little ants riding the leaf, picking harmful organisms
from our antennae, head, thorax, and abdomen;
that katydids and crickets stridulate. Like taking
a violin bow to string, they draw one wing
across the other, calling to their kind.
And just before the girl in a white lab coat
called us in with a lilting southern accent,
we learned there are over one million insect species
compared to four thousand mammals. "Maybe
that explains where all the human souls have gone,"
my soul mate whispered, before we went into the movie.

I guess it was the violin, talk of souls, rows of seats
leading to the front. Anyway, waiting for the film,
I thought of Susie Parker rising from her school bus seat,
her violin case held high, chestnut-colored ponytail
almost to her waist. Susie, walking down the aisle
ahead of me. Mr. Grunwald saying, "Careful now,"
pulling the robotic handle, opening the door.
Susie, walking down the steps and turning left.
"See ya," Susie said, about to cross the street.
"See ya," I said as I walked straight
from steps to street to sidewalk to my yard,
turning at the scream of tires, the thump of grill,
running to the sight of Susie. Violin open to the air.

Dolphins talk in clicks, click streams, and whistles.
Feeding on a giant ball of living fish,
dolphins communicate with spiraling bodies. One by one,
on signal, they thrust into the mass and feed
while the other dolphins keep the ball intact
like oceanic cowboys. Off a British West Indies island,
a solitary dolphin, JoJo, waits for Dean Bernal,
JoJo's only known companion. Dean swims
to JoJo every day, across the turquoise water.
There they speak in loops and spirals, sometimes touching.
When Dean listens closely, the quivering chords
in JoJo's larynx whistle just for him.

Standing in our hallway, outside the bathroom door,
I heard the woman sobbing. I heard the woman moan,
the woman who could not stop her large blue car.
Looking down the hallway, I saw my mother—her hair
longer, darker than today—her hand held out to me.
Mother led me to our pale green wing-backed chair
in the corner by the window. From there, I heard
the bathroom pocket door begin to slide.

When the woman joined my mother by our fireplace,
my mother took the woman in her arms.
From that chair, in that living room, I learned
the single sound two crying women make
as their skirts sway side to side in unison.

In the Blue Box

In the last thirty days I have finally found
a reliable concrete man to patch our driveway.
I have called a noted arborist to diagnose
the sickly dogwood tree in our backyard.
I've taken my uncle to the grocery
and our beagle to a chiropractor.
I have driven to a bookstore to purchase
a birthday card for my wife
and to my mother's apartment
when she didn't answer my call that morning.
I have obeyed my chest-congested, slightly confused,
eighty-five-year-old mother, leaving her alone
when she gasped, "I don't want you to see me this way"—
meaning she'd overslept and not dressed,
fixed her hair, or put on make-up. I have driven home,
cleaned my neglected office, and rested on my sun porch,
where half-way through a cup of coffee
I remembered to give my mother another call,
this time finding her too breathless to speak.
I've bounded up fifteen steps,
forced her down as many, and witnessed
what I feared to be her final breath—
her head drooping like a wilted flower in my car.
I have run a red light, zoomed
into my smooth, newly-repaired driveway,
and given my mother chest compressions
while my wife breathed into her mouth.

I've called my sister in Illinois, my brother in Oregon,
and repeated my mother's instructions
to an ER doctor who removed a breathing tube.
I have seen our redbud bud, azaleas bloom,
and my mother in an ICU come miraculously to.

I have had my hair cut.
I've eaten a birthday dinner with my wife
and tuna sandwiches in the hospital lunchroom with my sister.
I've discovered how to lose weight,
the pleasures of caffeine, and my mother
alone in her hospital room after a massive stroke.
I have seen pain in her eyes when she mumbled,
"I'm sorry you have to see me like this"
and joy when they opened for a last time to her children.
"I've had a wonderful life," my mother said.

I have been stood up by the noted arborist
and tapped on the shoulder by a funeral home director
at the mausoleum service. "I'm sorry to tell you," he said,
"but the cemetery says you owe another dollar ten cents."

I have felt the joy of anger being released.

I've ridden in the back seat of a hearse
and driven my five-time married, terminally-ill uncle
to divorce court in his Chevy van, stopping
only to snatch a wheelchair ("A wide one!"
he commanded) from an unattended clinic foyer.
I have pushed my uncle in a stolen wheelchair
past security into a courtroom.
I've eased him into a recliner in his den—
his feet the size of cantaloupes, legs thin as vines,
a snake of tube uncoiling from his nose
to a tank of gurgling oxygen in the hall.
"Life," I heard my uncle say
as my cousin Julie stepped into his kitchen.
"Life," I heard him say again.
"In the blue box. And with peaches."

I've written one obituary, two eulogies, a large check,
twenty-four thank you notes, about that many e-mails,
and I've almost called my mother on the phone
at least three times. In the last thirty days,
I have seen our dogwood clench its leaves like fists.

King of Albania

Lately, I've been thinking about Otto Witte—
German lion tamer/circus acrobat whose extraordinary magic skills
earned him an honorary chieftainship in an African Pygmy tribe
before he eloped with the Emperor of Ethiopia's daughter. Otto,
who in 1913, sword-swallowing his way through the Balkans,
discovered he resembled a certain Turkish prince
whom Albanian Moslems had asked to be their king—
Otto's cue to grab a uniform, pin some medals,
and proclaim himself King Otto I
before declaring war on Montenegro,
raiding the treasury and escaping the country.

                                                        Or so he claimed—
all the way to his not-at-all bitter end
in a Hamburg home for the aged, where
Otto clung to his fantasies and an identity card
issued by well-meaning German police.

Otto Witte
Entertainer
Former King of Albania

I've been thinking about Otto Witte—
how we could all use a little *pseudologia fantastica*.
If only you believed you eloped with Ethiopian royalty,
that you ruled Albania, and Montenegrins feared you.
If only you believed you were happy.

Identity Theft

1.

It's June and I can't *WAIT* for our new crepe myrtle to bloom!
I've forgotten the variety of our new crepe myrtle.
I could ask my wife.
But by not knowing the name of our new crepe myrtle,
I don't know the color of its blooms—
which only *ADDS* to my excitement! Not only that,
my wife said I could have another gazing ball—
to complement our new crepe myrtle!
Plus, we have a *CONSPICUOUS* gap in our hydrangeas!

I once climbed the Grand Teton.

2.

One day a man is walking his dog through a leafy park
when he sees a girl with a snake around her neck.
The snake's name is Noah. Noah the boa.
Only the man doesn't know Noah the boa's name
when he finds himself forming some *pret-ty* definite opinions
about the girl with purple-black hair and skin
the color of no color, excluding
the surfeit of tattoos, the gold and silver rings,
and pins on her pale canvas.
But the thing about this man, opinions or not,
he can't help but talk. In addition to Noah's name,
he learns Noah's body temperature approximates surrounding air,
so, no, Noah doesn't cool the girl on hot days. Surprisingly,
the girl works at the psychiatric hospital through the leafy trees
where she takes Noah on her days off to cheer the cheerless.
Also, Noah the 23-year-old affectionate boa
came from a Rosy Boa rescue,

which makes him feel not so rosy—the man—
since, now, *all* of his *pret-ty* definite opinions
are *pret-ty* definitely wrong.

Soon the man is expressing his displeasure
with the Frisbee golf course that violates the leafy trees,
when, despite their disparity in age, pets, skin tone, et cetera,
the girl suddenly says,
                      "I feel ya,"
to which the clueless man replies,
                                "Uh, no thanks."

Some days the man feels like a nameless crepe myrtle
that has forgotten the color of its blooms.

3.

My Grandma Mabel had an aunt named Myrtle.

4.

It's 1969. I'm at a Nashville honky-tonk with my friend Norman.
Norman and I are eighteen. In four years,
Norman will become a Nashville cop. One night
he'll pull me over in my Pinto and ask to see my license.
"Hey, Norman. It's me," I'll say. But tonight
Norman already has a license *and* a social security card
for one William B. Robinson, age 21-plus.
"Wh*Y,* you *bo-oys* have the *say-m nay-m!*"
our waitress says after careful study.
Norman will matriculate to Vanderbilt Law.
He'll become a prominent defense attorney.

"We're fraternal twins," Norman tells the waitress.
"I'm William Butler Robinson,
and he's my brother, William Blake."

"*Ye-ah,* and I'm Tammy *WY*-nette," the waitress says.

5.

My mother's maiden name was Angel. Martha Jeanne Angel.
"I was an angel before I met your dad," my mother liked to say.

6.

One day the man is stopped at a stoplight near the leafy park
(where he seems to spend a lot of time),
when he notices a girl in a giant red pick-up
with a young man's hands around her neck.
The young man's name is Tim, Tim as in
"Get your hands *off* me, Tim!" Once again,
the man finds himself forming some *pret-ty* definite opinions
when the girl jumps from the giant red pick-up
and starts running down the leafy street
and Tim jumps from the giant red pick-up
and starts running down the leafy street, too.
Naturally, the man can't help but talk.

But this time his talking must wait until the light turns green
and he drives around the block listening to someone say,
"You just can't drive away you miserable coward!"—
bearing in mind there is no one with him in his car.

Later that night he tells his wife what he *did* say
after he rounds the block and follows the re-occupied,
giant red pick-up to Emergency Parking at a nearby hospital—
which doesn't make the miserable coward feel any less miserable
or cowardly.

7.

Man: (*knocking on passenger-side window of a giant red pick-up*)

    Are you OK?

Girl: (*rolling down window*)

    Yes. Thanks.

Tim: (*jumping from driver's side of the giant red pick-up,
    siren blaring in the background*)

    Who the hell are you!

Man: I just want to make sure she's OK.

Tim: (*balling his fists*)

    You might want to leave us alone, m_____ f_____!

Man: I just want to make sure you're both OK.

LATER THAT DAY

Wife: (*watering blue hydrangeas*)

    He never would have hit someone your age.

8.

Some days it seems impossible to the man
that he is 23 in Rosy Boa years.
That no one will ever hit him hard right between the eyes.

9.

If you don't know me by now,
You will never never never know me, ooh, ooh-ooh-ooh-ooh.

10.

If the last 23 years were an illusion,
Simply Red would be singing "If You Don't Know Me By Now,"
Noah the boa would be about seven inches long,
and I would be showing this poem to my gentle friend and mentor,
the exquisite formalist poet, Mike Carson,
who would undoubtedly return it to me with the word *DECORUM!*
written in the right-hand margin of Part 7—
since I would have undoubtedly filled the blanks in.
Never mind Tim the angry, giant red pick-up driver,
or rather angry Tim, the giant—oh, you know what I mean—
filled the blanks in, too. Never mind Tim is not alive
and pick-ups aren't so giant.

If the last 23 years were *not* an illusion,
Tim *would* be alive, pick-ups *would* be giant,
and I'd be asking when you last heard the word *decorum?*
If you find it kind of nice to hear the word decorum
and wish there were precious more of it going around,
chances are you had a grandmother and great-great aunt
with names like Mabel and Myrtle. Chances are
you sometimes forget the color of your blooms.

11.

Some days I can't believe I've become someone
who longs for the days when more decorum was going around,
someone who uses *long* as a verb and *precious* at all.

Some days I can't believe my knees have wrinkles.
That I count lawn mowing as exercise.
That my mower is self-propelled.

Some days I can't believe I still say, *honky-tonk*.
That I plant blue hydrangeas.
That both my mother and my dad are angels now.

12.

It's 2012 and I'm at a funeral home telling my friend Norman
that I'm sorry about his mother, Pearl.
It's been many years since I've seen Norman. Of course
we'll talk about the time he pulled me over in my Pinto.
The time we hiked The Appalachian Trail.
(I once hiked The Appalachian Trail.)

"This is my friend William Blake Robinson,"
smiling Norman tells his granddaughter.
"It's nice to meet you Mr. Robinson,"
smiling Norman's smiling granddaughter says.

13.

One day in 1704, a man appeared in England.
He claimed to be Prince George Psalmanazar, reformed cannibal
from the island of Formosa—where men ate adulterous wives,
18,000 baby boys were sacrificed each year to an elephant god,
and everyone wore snakes around their necks
TO KEEP THEM COOL! Little wonder
A Historical and Geographical Description of Formosa,
An Island Subject to the Emperor of Japan was a bestseller.
When a Jesuit missionary from Formosa asked about his fair skin,
Psalmanazar claimed he'd always lived beneath the ground.
"Sunlight would shine directly down an equatorial chimney,"
the astronomer Edmond Halley reasoned.
"Formosan chimneys are almost always built at crooked angles
and containing bends," Psalmanazar rebutted.
"*Ye-ah*, and I'm Tammy *WY*-nette,"
Sir Edmond might as well have said.

14.

Well, I hit him hard right between the eyes
And he went down, but to my surprise,
He come up with a knife and cut off a piece a my ear.

15.

If the last 43 years were an illusion,
Johnny Cash would be singing "A Boy Named Sue"
on the jukebox in the Nashville honky-tonk
where I'm drinking beer with my friend Norman,
thanks to the likes of Tammy Wynette.
In four years, I'll get a job in a psychiatric hospital
and acquire a life-long soft spot for those who cheer the cheerless.
After that, I'll climb the Grand Teton, hike The Appalachian Trail,
and develop an interest in ornamental shrubbery—
which will lead to a delight in gazing balls.
One day I'll gaze into my favorite,
the deep blue ball with light green swirls.

I'll find it hard to believe I've become someone
who gazes into a deep blue ball with light green swirls,
especially with the likes of William Blake
drinking Old Milwaukee Beer in a Nashville honky-tonk,
signaling to Tammy Wynette but gazing out at me
and saying,
         "Who the hell are you?"

Mr. Know-It-All

For forty years, this   *friend of mine,*
                          this know-it-all *friend of mine,*
has sung along with the radio:

  "Baby, I'm amazed at the way I really need you,"

unaware that *maybe,* not *baby*
he should be amazed at the way he really needs her—
fair warning that *maybe* he doesn't know everything. Still,
one day Mr. Know-It-All is driving home
when he's forced to stop at a fallen tree limb,
and a young man somewhere between the ages of fifteen and thirty
steps out from behind a giant catalpa tree
and drags the limb into the gutter.

Pulling up alongside the young man, window up,
Mr. Know-It-All gives the OK sign with his left hand—
his habit for the past sixty-six years (I have reason to know)—
though the young man seems to have no idea
what Mr. Know-It-All is doing, the young man's right hand
replying with a kind of slow, mid-air somersault
before landing in a peace sign, victory sign, whatever,
at which time Mr. Know-It-All feels compelled
to roll the window down and say, "Did you know
that sign originated in 1415 at the Battle of Agincourt
when victorious English archers flashed their two bow fingers
at the French—fingers the French had promised to cut off?"

"Cool," the young man says.

Then, this same know-it-all *friend*—who feels a little guilty
about not helping drag the limb into the gutter (he tells me)—
discovers The Battle of Agincourt was fought in late October,
a time the show-off archers' fingers
would be cool in northern France, something
Mr. Know-It-All would like to tell the kind young man
(I know for sure).

So, the other morning when my alarm goes off
and I not so much rise from bed as stumble, fall into my jeans,
let the dogs into the yard, and start coffee
with the sinking feeling I did all this about an hour ago
and how I will do it again in another insignificant hour
and then the insignificant hour after that and that, et cetera,
I'm not surprised when Mr. Know-It-All shows up
and takes *my* seat at the kitchen table. "Life
is a regular Orffyreus Wheel, don't you think?" he asks.

And though I have a pretty good idea where he's going with this,
I have a very good idea he'll continue:

"In 1717, Johann Bessler, aka Orffyreus,
placed a wheel twelve feet in diameter, fourteen inches thick—
its inner workings sealed from view with canvas—
in a locked room in Weissenstein Castle, where, inexplicably,
the wheel kept going round. Two months later,
Orffyreus came into the room and smashed
his perpetually-spinning wheel to bits. Only then
did he realize how much he'd miss it. Life
is a regular Orffyreus Wheel, don't you think?"
Mr. Know-It-All repeats, when I hear my wife,
DeeGee, walking down the hall.

"You asked me that already, Mr. Know-It-All," I say. "By the way, didn't Mrs. Orffyreus sometimes sneak into the castle room and give the wheel a push?"

"Baby," Mr. Know-It-All says. "*J u s t* baby."

Speaking of Tongues

You must be sober! You must be sincere! You must work for earnest! You must obey! I have spoken.
   Who the hell is Ernest?
from *Unbroken*: A World War II Story of Survival, Resilience, and Redemption
—by Laura Hillenbrand

Who would have thought the *log roll* I learned in fifth-grade gym
would come in handy as I make my way beneath our ductwork,
our bathroom pipes, on my semi-annual, fully-dreaded
crawl space inspection—legs straight, knees pressed,
arms locked above my head?

My termite guy, Chuck, always wears a helmet.
*Un*protected, rolling on Visqueen-covered pea gravel
toward the darkness beneath our sun porch,
I'm struck by visions of a Pentecostal church in Nashville,
where the log roll—and variations of it—held sway. Sway
being the right word as all around me, people did just that,
some with the red-headed preacher's hand against their foreheads,
others swaying on their own to his unintelligible tongue
before they dropped and rolled around Samantha O'Rourke
and me—Samantha, the girl whose long blonde hair
graced the hardwood floor of our Nineteenth Century
British and American Poetry class whenever,
two rows up, she leaned back into her seat. Samantha
who agreed to grace me with her presence on a date
if I agreed to grace her Friday service first.
                              "What did you think?"
she asked as we settled into my Pinto.

   "*'Twas brillig, and the slithy toves
   Did gyre and gimble in the wabe:*"

                              foolishly I said.

Beware the Jubjub bird, and shun
The frumious Bandersnatch!

                                                                                         she must have been thinking
as she said in completely *in*telligible terms, No,
she did not want to go to Rotier's Bar for a drink,
and, "Please take me back to my quadrangle now!"

                        *

Rule number one for crawl space inspection is:

    SHUT THE DOOR BEHIND YOU!

The last thing you want to happen
is to find yourself in a crawl space with a cat.
Your neighbor's unaltered cat.

His name was Teddy.

But *this* time I've rolled safely to the space beneath our kitchen,
checking the sink for leaks and—speaking of tongues—
thinking of the time my mother swallowed hers.

1965: a time when every fourteen-year-old boy
is letting his flat-top grow and playing a guitar, a drum set,
or, in my case, a not-so-portable Hammond organ,
with hopes of securing a spot in a band and the hand of a girl.

It's my birthday. I'm celebrating with my band, The Customs,
with a living room performance of our hits, when
my girlfriend calls to say she's met someone else,
an excellent time to focus on our drummer's girlfriend,
Mary Lou Headley, I decide.

I'm blasting out dominant chords to beat my band,
looking Mary Lou straight in the eye while singing,

   "Wooly bully, wooly bully,"

when out of the side of my eye,
I see my mother drop.

Underneath my sun porch, I'm somewhere below
our loveseat glider and my dog-eared copy of *Unbroken,*
thinking of my parents and their forty-four-year marriage
that, unlike Louis Zamperini, was not unbroken or resilient,
and how their bodies—in separate vaults
at Park Lawn Mausoleum, Patrician Chapel—
are under one roof but in separate rooms again.

But more importantly, I'm thinking of how my father
rushed into the silenced living room, tilted
my mother's head and reached into her throat
while murmuring a kind of language
I had never heard him speak—as she began to breathe,
to look into my father's eyes, to smile,
and murmur something back.

Voyagers

My dad and his business partner, Ed, were standing in their office
when their friend Frank walked in. They laughed. They talked.
"What are your other kids doing, Paul?" Frank asked my father.
"Paula is a CPA in Chicago. Scott's in engineering at Purdue."
Ed turned to Dad and said, "Two out of three isn't bad."

And yes, I *was* there, wearing one of my five polyester leisure suits
(one for each workday), perhaps my favorite, lime green,
which went with all of my pastel turtlenecks, each neck
hidden by a beard that won't become fashionable for forty years.
An impediment to real estate sales, I see now.

But if you had been an English major with a minor in psychology
and your father said, "Come home and work for me," when you
were playing 5-card draw, shooting bumper pool, and pinning
psychiatric patients to the floor in Nashville,
you might have come home, too, you

with your undergrad accomplishments: your American Lit paper,
"Pip Squeaks," where the mad cabin boy in *Moby Dick* says,
"Cook! Ho, coo! and cook us! Jenny! Hey, hey, hey;"
your knowledge of fellow Hoosier, Kurt Vonnegut; and
the psych study you conducted, "A Glance at Eye Contact."

"*I cannot tell why it was . . . that those stage managers, the Fates,
put me down for this shabby part of a whaling voyage,*
began Pip's crew-mate, Ishmael. And though I don't mean to imply
that playing backgammon with fellow salesman, Dick Romerhaus,
as in "Picture a house roaming around" Romerhaus, interspersed

with infrequent showings and yet more infrequent house sales
compared to a *shabby part of a whaling voyage,* I do wonder
what would have happened to me if I hadn't come home.

The World Series of Poker? A career in bumper pool?
Professional wrestling?

The best pool player I ever played was my uncle Bill. A POW
in World War II, he lost fifty pounds and all of his teeth.
When he came home, he was hit by a train. He lived.
"I'm a lucky man," he'd grin. No one told a joke like him.
No one would have enjoyed his funeral more than he.

"Luck, good or bad, is not the hand of God," said interplanetary
traveler Winston Niles Rumford in *The Sirens of Titan*.
*"Luck is the way the wind swirls and the dust settles
eons after God has passed by."* At Saint Joseph Cemetery,
my uncle's honor guard showed up without a bugler. Instead,

they brought a boom box. But first, they fired the guns.
And soon, they'd fold a flag and hand it to my cousin Gary.
When the war ended and the Germans opened the camp gates,
Uncle Bill, less than a hundred pounds by then, walked
across Czechoslovakia in search of Americans. At the cemetery,

we'd thought my uncle's wind had finished swirling.
But before his dust settled, with his family and friends
gathered solemnly around, the *bugler* pushed a button.
You should have seen the look on that man's face when,
instead of "Taps," the box boomed "Reveille."

In a Bed of Purple Iris

    Soon, DeeGee will have "that awful camera test," a test
that will determine whether we spend the next several months
       building a house with rounded interior corners,
   two sky lights
      ("flared," she insists),
and archway to the sun porch of our dreams

    or making visits to Oncology/Hematology Associates.
With help from Gardar Gislason, a slim Teutonic doctor
      with red, close-shaven hair
   and blue-green eyes,
      I am able to imagine
my slim blonde wife lying on her side

    wearing a hospital gown of indistinct floral print
while he threads a little camera through her pancreas,
      via throat, esophagus,
   stomach, and bile duct.
      Meanwhile, I will sit
with strangers in the surgery waiting room,

    sipping coffee, exchanging smiles. But for now,
I am sitting in my rocking chair, a tabby cat
      the color of autumn leaves
   purring at my head
      as DeeGee passes by my chair again—
on her way from our bedroom, through our den,

    and out our back door—balancing a sheet of notebook paper
upon which she carries two or three rust-red ants each trip,
      carefully kneeling
   in a bed of purple iris
      outside an open window. "Stay out here," she says.
And one time, "This is your new home."

2

Fred's Theory of Relativity

"Stupid is as stupid does," said Forest Gump. So true.
Like the time nine-year-old me, batting eighth,
squared around to bunt and took a Larry Broerman
fastball in the groin that dropped me to the ground,
where the coaches and umps huddled around
and unbuttoned my pants so I could breathe.
A button I forgot to button before trotting,
halfway, to first base.

Ten years later, I leaned my pale neck
from a car window and yelled at every
white person I passed in downtown Birmingham.
If only I had shouted, "Roll Tide" or "War Eagle"
or sung, "Sweet Home Alabama"
instead of shouting, "Red neck, red neck!"
the BPD officer might have let me pass through.

Stupider.

*

The only thing that got me through college
was an average ability to write papers.
So, when my roommate and I
were assigned a paper for Philosophy 101,
I got busy. A week later, around midnight,
the night before the paper was due, Fred began.

My paper: C

Fred's Theory of Relativity: A-

*

Last Friday, as my wife, DeeGee and our friend Va
canvassed for city council candidates
in a neighborhood filled with *No Soliciting,
No Trespassing,* and *Beware of Dog* signs,
I followed in the car, providing muscle.

Me: brave

Last Sunday, at Fred's funeral visitation,
after telling his wife, Cathy and her son Frederick
about Fred's paper, I asked Frederick,
whose job at SpaceX is to formulate a fuel
from Martian ice, soil, and/or air for the return trip,
"Have you come up with a way to get us back?"

"Maybe not the first guy,"
said Frederick with Fred's grin.

Astronauts: braver

                          *

You were a good guy, Fred. Remember those nights
when I finished studying and I'd say,
"Let's go have a beer"?

"There's nothing you could say that would convince me.
Not one thing. I have work to do," you'd say.

"Fred?" I'd argue.

"OK."

Remember jumping on the trampoline
in your family's living room,
leaving handprints on the ceiling?

You were a smart guy, Fred—
you with your law degree.

Me with my real estate license.

You with that A-.

My guess is that you return for Cathy every day
in every room of her house. Hey, Fred,
next time, help Cathy look for your paper.
She said you kept a lot of stuff from school.
She said she'd like to read your theory. Me, too.
I'd like to see what you knew then—

and know what you know now.

Has Becky Wright Returned
A Prayer for Owen Meany?

"Check the bookcase in the foyer," says DeeGee. I do.
Anna Karenina, Olive Kitteridge. No *Owen Meany*.
A book I read in high school. And there,
one I read in Colorado—summer, 1971,
when I told the youth camp wrangler,
"I've ridden all my life," and he hired me.

In fact, my experience was zero.
Zero: also the chance I gave the screaming girl
lying helpless on the ground beside her saddle,
a saddle I had cinched. Meanwhile,
half-a-dozen horses thundered toward her.

Daughter of Fortune, The Lovely Bones. No *Owen Meany*.

*

Zero was my number on our fifth-grade basketball team.
"Don't be a hero, Zero!" a parent shouted
as I ran onto the court.

"Why can't I have a real number?"
I pled with Coach Fitzsimmons. "Mark,
zero is a placeholder,
and it's holding you a place on the team."
Zero: the points I often scored.

"What's this book about?" I ask DeeGee. *"The Piano Tuner."*

"It's about a piano tuner who goes somewhere.
Burma, I think. I remember liking him."

Every few years, I read *A Prayer for Owen Meany*.
It gives me hope that we are here for a reason,
or, to be honest, that *I* am here for a reason,
that the things I do each day—like rummaging
around a bookcase before retiring to my chair;
light lunch, quick nap; an afternoon of writing
and a sunset spin on my stationary bike—
prepare me for   THE ACT   I am destined to perform.

That I am not your run-of-the-mill placeholder.
At least not for much longer.

The Reader, *The Hero with a Thousand Faces*.
No *Owen Meany*.

             *

My friend Greg Griggs is a piano tuner. Plus,
Greg and his wife, Tracee, go somewhere:
Florida, usually, Costa Rica, twice. Unlike Owen Meany,
Greg has never placed a live grenade
onto an airport bathroom windowsill
to save a planeload of Vietnamese children.
He would have mentioned it, I am sure.
But if your life depends upon a tuned piano,
Greg's your man.

    A-Sharp Piano Services

or as I call it:

    B-Flat Piano Services

"Smart ass," Greg says, grinning.

You will remember liking him.

*

>   *for God will deigne*
> *To visit oft the dwellings of just Men*
> *Delighted, and with frequent intercourse*
> *Thither will send his winged Messengers*
> *On errands of supernal Grace,*

wrote John Milton in *Paradise Lost,*
which can also be found in our bookcase.

Next to my chair, just beyond my stationary bike,
is a window. Just outside the window, a beautiful redbud tree,
the perfect spot for a winged messenger to alight, I'd think.

I will be the guy awaiting instructions,
holding place in his chair.

With or without *Owen Meany*.

*

We live our lives in the hope of finding *Owen Meany*—
that part of us that runs onto the court,
into an airport bathroom, or wherever
and is a hero.

A few months ago, I was at a funeral home
talking to my friend Bill, whose dad, Big Bill, had died.
Suddenly, Little Bill turns to speak to someone else,
and I'm alone with his wife—Charlotte,
I think it is. Charlene, maybe Sharon. I'm babbling
on about the things Big Bill accomplished
(as if she doesn't know), when she says, "Yes,
my Bill has some large shoes to fill." And I say,
"Maybe he should just fill his own shoes."
Then Charlotte, Charlene, or maybe Sharon says,
"You're right. And he only wears a 9."

Clarence Darrow for the Defense,
As I Lay Dying. Still, no *Owen Meany.*

                    *

"You were right," I say. "Says here on the back cover
that the piano tuner goes to Burma."

"That's what I thought," says DeeGee.
"He leaves his wife in England," she huffs.

"I thought you remembered liking him."

"Except for that," she says.

                                   I could do worse—
not that I would leave DeeGee in England.
Yet who knows, someone someday might say,
"Old what's-his-name, didn't know a rat's ass about horses.
Almost got a poor girl killed.

"Terrible basketball player. As for his writing, well,
he never used one word when ten words would do,
ever.

"But hey, the guy could read all day.
Heck of a stationary bike rider!
Had a beautiful redbud tree.

"Some might say he went somewhere.
I remember liking him. And, oh yeah,
he had *some* book collection:

*"Book of the Dead, Deliverance,
A Prayer for Owen Meany."*

Stripping Down to Fundamentalists

It's because I know the world is absurd that I'm not going to kill you. But if I somehow figure out that the world has meaning, I can kill you in the name of that meaning.
   —Kamel Daoud, author of The Meursault Investigation,
      a retelling of The Stranger by Albert Camus

Dear Kamel,

Today as I was driving—with Bodhi Day, Pancha Ganapati,
Hanukkah, Kwanzaa, and Christmas around the corner—
I remembered your interview on NPR. You might be right.
The best of all possible worlds would be one without meaning:
no one ready to defend their beliefs at the drop of a turban, kufi,
or yarmulke. Still, some of us have to get out of bed every day.
Might it be a good thing to have something to get out of bed for—
a meaning, if you will? Yes, I know this is where the trouble starts.
Take publisher, Larry Flynt, secure in his belief to make money,
only to spend *lots* of money ($3,000,000)
to protect his right to parody Reverend Jerry Falwell
in a *Hustler* issue I don't feel comfortable discussing.
But Jerry Falwell had some beliefs, too. Let's just say
that his beliefs and Larry Flynt's beliefs
had about as much in common as Christmas and April Fools
(not that Larry is one). Did they kill each other? No. Did they
travel around the country debating 1st Amendment rights issues
while agreeing to agree they'd never agree on anything? Yes.

"I am a Christian," said Jerry Falwell.
"Smut is my vocation," said Larry Flynt.

                              The thing is, Kamel,
if an evangelist and a smut peddler can become friends—
exchange dieting tips, share pictures of their grandchildren,

talk about the days Jerry's father bootlegged in Virginia
(a trade Larry once practiced in Kentucky)—
maybe the rest of us can, too. Get along, I mean.
My favorite part of *The Meursault Investigation*
is when Musa puts his little brother, Harun, on his shoulders,
and Harun grabs Musa's ears, steering his head while Musa
rolls a tire down the street and makes a sound like a motor.
They could be brothers anywhere. Anyway,
good luck with your book. And if you ever leave Algeria
for southern Indiana, look me up. Don't be a stranger.

Fractals

> *A cloud is made of billows upon billows upon billows that look like clouds. As you come closer to a cloud, you get not something smooth but irregularities on a smaller scale.*
> —Benoit Mandelbrot

July 4, 1973. I'm the guy driving the blue Ford Pinto
with the flammable hatchback and white vinyl top,
a top which will give me cleaning fits for the next ten years
before it turns gray and I sell the car to a woman who will claim,
"A Pinto saved my life!"
                    Lucky for me,
she will be broadsided, not rear-ended, in her combustible engine
soon after my buddy Bob (that's him in the passenger seat)
and I celebrate college graduation with this trip to Maine.

But we have far to go.

That's Indiana in the background.

*

You can tell it's Indiana by the number of cars with Indiana plates.
Otherwise, it looks a lot like Illinois:
corn, soybeans, Howard Johnson's.

> *I've seen every highway in the United States by now, and they all look alike to me.*
> —Loretta Lynn

In 1975, Benoit Mandelbrot will notice
that if you break certain geometric shapes into pieces,
the little pieces look pretty much like the big shape.
And if you break the little pieces into littler pieces,
the littler pieces look pretty much like the little pieces.

                                                    And so on . . .

He'll call the shape a *fractal*.

The road from Saint Louis through Ohio is a fractal.
But I don't know that yet. It's still 1973.
Benoit is at IBM, busy figuring,
as Bob and I exit I-70 into a small Ohio town that—
with the exception of the parade
we suddenly find ourselves wedged in—
looks like all the other Illinois, Indiana, and Ohio towns
we have exited into.

This time Bob is driving.
That's us behind the fire truck.

And that's the melody from "American Pie"
carried haltingly by the trombone section
in the marching band behind us.

                        *

On May 19, 1979, I will stagger through mile twenty-six
and step onto a quarter-mile cinder track
with about fifteen other straggling runners:
                                    a kind of sad parade.

  Ah, ha, ha, ha, stayin' alive, stayin' alive,

                                a cruel loudspeaker will sing
as I limp across the finish line into a canvas recovery tent,
where I will notice a slender, fair-haired girl
recovering from her run with the aid of a cigarette.

The beautiful girl will not notice me.

But in *this* parade the Buckeye girls who line the street
can't seem to get enough of Bob and me, cheering wildly,
wildly waving as we pass—
the two of us doing our best parade waves
through the open windows of my Pinto, in return.

*

Clouds, snowflakes, certain animal-coloration patterns
                              (a leopard comes to mind),
broccoli, cauliflower:
                    fractals all.

Lungs, pulmonary vessels. Galaxies!

That's Bob and me on top of Cadillac Mountain,
stuffed with wild blueberries we've consumed along the trail.
We're looking at Maine's coastline.
In a few years I'll learn it's a fractal, too,
along with ocean waves parading toward shore.

Lightning bolts. Also fractals.

But I won't be thinking about that either—
after we descend Cadillac Mountain
and the rain and lightning start for real
and we realize no way will our pathetic little tent protect us
like a cozy bar in Bar Harbor and a beautiful girl or two
who can't wait to take us to their cozy home
from a *bah* in *Bah Hahba* would.

What a magnificent coastline!

        *

Here are some things I remember from that night:

1) driving into Bar Harbor in a downpour;
2) naming lobsters (Larry, Louie, Lonnie, et cetera)
    swimming in a restaurant tank
3) watching paramedics revive a cook who *in*haled
    while priming a propane cookstove with a rubber straw;
4) eating lobster (Larry) for the first time;
5) deciding never to name another meal;
6) walking into a bar on Mt. Desert Street
    and seeing a slender, fair-haired girl smoking a cigarette—
    alone;
7) noticing the beautiful girl did not notice me;
8) noticing the Bunyanesque, black-and-red plaid figure
    who suddenly eclipsed the bar's doorframe
    did notice Bob and me sitting at a table
    with his slender, fair-haired girlfriend, Uta—
    Uta having already described the *ahgument*
    she and Little Jack had earlier that day;
9) slow dancing with Uta to "A Whiter Shade of Pale"—
    with Little Jack's permission
10) a lava lamp.

        *

Here are some lines from a poem called "Relax," by Ellen Bass.

> *Your parents will die.*
> *No matter how many vitamins you take,*
> *how much Pilates, you'll lose your keys,*
> *your hair, and your memory.*

And then:

> *Your wallet will be stolen, you'll get fat,*
> *slip on the bathroom tiles of a foreign hotel*
> *and crack your hip.*

Except for the hotel part, Ellen has me pegged.

Could we all be little pieces?

Chips off the Old Block?

*

Here are some fairly accurate lines from a bar in Bar Harbor.

Little Jack: One time th' snow was so frickin' deep, I stubbed my toe on th' top of a telephone pole!

Me: No kidding.

Little Jack: One time we used a *puhtato* for a football!

Bob: No kidding.

Uta: These guys need a place to stay tonight.

Little Jack: One time I walked into a *bah* and found two
                guys hittin' on my girlfriend. I gave 'em a choice.
                They could buy me *beeyah* for th' rest a th' night—
                and I'd give 'em a place to stay—or we could
                go outside and settle up *anathah* way! *Ayuh.*

Me: Oh, bartender.

*

Dear Uta,

I'm the guy who was driving the blue Ford Pinto
with the white vinyl top, the guy who followed
you and Little Jack home in what he called a "wicked *pissah"*
forty years ago. The other guy was Bob.
I hope you and Little Jack are having good lives.
(Perhaps there are Littler Jacks and/or Small Jills.) More
than likely, your life has seemed a succession of small parades.
Chances are your parents have died and you've lost your keys.
Uta, does the world sometimes look like it's slipped
on the bathroom tiles of a foreign hotel and cracked
into 7,173,302,544 angry little pieces? Anyway,
I just wish everyone could get along as well today
as the four of us did that night.
("We skipped the light fandango," didn't we, Uta?) After all,
we want the same things: a nice meal, a drink or two, some music,
and someone to share the meal, the drinks, and music with.
Plus, a dry roof above our heads. You might say
we are but irregularities at a smaller scale.

A belated thanks, Uta. My best to you and Little Jack.
And if you missed something from your kitchen that next morning,
please forgive me.

Though it was Bob's idea.

*

Sunrise: July 8, 1973. That's Bob and me
waking up on Little Jack and Uta's screened porch.
In Yorktown Heights, New York, for all I know
Benoit Mandelbrot is measuring broccoli florets in his sleep.
But in our sleeping bags, Bob and I
are figuring the odds of a sober Little Jack
appreciating us as much on his porch this morning
as he did in his favorite *bah* last night.

Predictably, we will rise.
Sadly, we'll sneak into the kitchen and snatch an orange.
In my Pinto, Bob will peel the orange and ask me to slow down
so he can toss the rind into the harbor.
"For Larry's cousins," Bob will say.

Bob will break the orange in half.
We'll break our halves into littler pieces,
pop them, one by one, into our mouths,
                                      and drive away.

*

July 10, 1973. That's my Pinto pulling out of Stuckey's,
where Bob and I bought four Pecan Log Rolls
and two packages of Pecan Divinity—
to repay our parents for college educations.

Bob will marry Jeannine, a French tennis player.
I'll marry DeeGee, the fair-haired runner
who will finally notice *me* at another sad parade.

But for now, that's Pennsylvania in the background.
From a distance, it's hard to say which guy is Bob
and which is me.

Aspirations

It is almost unbelievable that the insects should have undergone
several stages of metamorphosis within the sinuses.
—Paul D. Hurd Jr., *Science,* June 1954

Summer, 1953.
Paul D. Hurd Jr. is in Point Barrow, Alaska,
collecting bees with an aspirator, a device
consisting of a stoppered vial, two copper tubes,
a rubber tube, a fine-mesh brass screen, and two lips (his),
unaware that, a few months from now,
three adult rove beetles, thirteen fungus gnat larvae,
three egg parasite wasps, and fifty springtails
will crawl, ooze, fly, and spring from his nose
and make their new home in California.

This is how life works. You go to Alaska to collect bees,
and you wind up with adult rove beetles in California.
Or, in the case of the painter Samuel F. B. Morse, you go
to Paris with aspirations of becoming America's Rembrandt,
spending two years in the gallery of the Louvre
painting (what else?) *The Gallery of the Louvre,*
until one day you take a walk outside Paris
and notice flag-waving Frenchmen atop wooden towers,
and you wind up in New York inventing the telegraph.

Or you're me, and you spend the late 1970's aspiring
to qualify for the 1980 Olympic Marathon Trials—as likely
as a fungus gnat larva metamorphosing into a parasite wasp—
when you find yourself somewhere over the Caribbean
in a Cessna Golden Eagle with Elliott, your rich, octogenarian pilot
who has organized *The International Saint Kitts Half Marathon,*
"International" meaning a few guys from Nevis,
two or three from Trinidad, three hundred
or so Kittitians, and the five of you
from Elliott's hometown in Indiana

on your way to race a lap around the island,
your plane a tiny, smooth-gliding silhouette
on the aquamarine waters below
until you lose what seems a thousand feet
in the time it takes Elliott to turn toward you and yell,

> "GRAB SOME LUGGAGE TO EJECT!
> WE'RE GOING DOWN!"

*

In his 1974 classic, *Zen and the Art of Motorcycle Maintenance*,
Robert Pirsig writes,

> *You look at where you're going and where you are*
> *and it never makes sense, but then you look back*
> *at where you've been, and a pattern seems to emerge.*

And though I would not call it a particularly clear pattern,
I can make out a line weaving through a second career,
a new house, a wedding, a first career, and there, somewhere
between Fort Lauderdale and San Juan, Puerto Rico,
a falling Cessna Golden Eagle with me stuffing my copy of *Zen
and the Art of Motorcycle Maintenance* into my red backpack
as Elliott's laughter dawns on me like a Caribbean sunrise.

But here in an adult rove beetle stage—and then some—
life makes as much sense as sucking bees
in a Point Barrow meadow or sitting
in the gallery of the Louvre, painting thirty-eight teeny replicas
of the masterworks around you on one canvas. Then again,

it's more like *walking* beneath fierce equatorial sunlight
through the 10-mile mark of a 13-mile footrace
just before a kind Saint Kitts woman offers you a cup of water
and you stop to take a sip and then
                                a breath.

Pep Talks, The Movie

*If you want a happy ending, that depends,
of course, on where you stop the story.*
—Orson Welles

Cast (in order of appearance)

Mark Williams	Paul Giamatti
Sophie the beagle	Sophie the beagle
Coach 2	J. K. Simmons
Beth Ann Baumgart	Roseanne Barr
John Adams	Paul Giamatti
Abigail Adams	Laura Linney
teenage Mark Williams	Daniel Radcliffe
teenage Beth Ann Baumgart	Kiera Knightley
Olive Littlejohn	Helen Mirren
John Heisman	J. K. Simmons
Joey the parakeet	Pete the parakeet
Daniel Boone	Fess Parker III
Simon the hound	Sophie the beagle
DeeGee Williams	Laura Linney
Zach-the-ER-Doc	Steve Nash and Emily Dickinson

Boonville, Indiana—Spring 2017

FADE IN: white Honda CRV

That's me driving through Boonville, Indiana, the town
where Lincoln learned the law and Daniel Boone never set foot.
That's my arthritic beagle, Sophie, in the seat beside me.
And there's a cop-wanna-be *ZOOOMING!* by on a motorcycle
followed by a hearse with the plate *COACH 2*. I pull over.

"Coach 2?" I puzzle aloud to Sophie as a Pontiac Aztec, a blue
Chevy van and a yellow Charger complete the procession.

"Must be an assistant coach . . . Boonville Pioneers . . .
driving a hearse in the off-season," I explain,
when it dawns on me, the funeral home owns two *coaches*!

Even so, I imagine Coach 2 *is* driving—
the head coach assigned to a more important funeral—
and now it's up to Coach 2 to give a final pep talk
to someone with a friend who drives an Aztec.
Orange. (VOICEOVER: Coach 2)

"This is the most important game you'll ever play.
Just remember, *life* is the hard part. But that's behind you now.
So get in there and have some fun! On three:
One, two, three. Go Pioneer!"
(CUE: Sophie snoring)

Evansville, Indiana—Fall 2009

Here I am in the Thunderbolt Room at the Holiday Inn,
surrounded by a hundred aging high school classmates.
That's Beth Ann Baumgart, whom I haven't seen in forty years.
Beth Ann's been either importing or exporting
in Boston or New York, if I heard her right,
while I remained in southern Indiana.

We are sipping a sweet Chablis from plastic Dixie cups
when Beth Ann says to me,

                    "You sell real estate? Here?
I always thought you'd *do* something."

Philadelphia, Pennsylvania—July 2, 1776

One day after declaring Independence
and sending Thomas Jefferson off to put it into writing,
John Adams is seated at a desk, quill in hand,
room flickering in candlelight . . .

FADE IN: Abigail Adams, seated at a desk, letter in hand
VOICEOVER: John Adams

Dear Abigail,

The Second Day of July 1776 will be the most memorable Epocha in the History of America. I am apt to believe it will be celebrated by succeeding generations as the great anniversary Festival. It ought to be solemnized with Pomp and Parade, with Shews, Games, Sports. Guns, Bells, Bonfires, and Illuminations from one End of this Continent to the other from this Time forward forever more!

> *Your admiring Husband,*
> *John*

Evansville, Indiana—Spring 1968

That's me seated at a knife-ravaged school desk
in a rickety upstairs classroom at Central High,
the oldest operating high school west of the Appalachians—
where Daniel Boone never set foot. I'm taking
the college entrance exams with my eyes on Beth Ann Baumgart,
one desk up. What follows?

A) I panic when I notice all others have put down their pencils.
B) Weeks later, I'm summoned to the office of Senior Counselor, Olive Littlejohn (FADE IN: Olive Littlejohn, seated at desk, results in hand). "You'll never go to college now!" she says.
C) I consider a life of refrigerator assembly at the Whirlpool plant. (FADE IN: Whirlpool plant)
D) All of the above.

Atlanta, Georgia—October 7, 1916

With Georgia Tech leading Cumberland College 126 to 0,
Tech football coach, John Heisman (yes, that Heisman),
says to his team at halftime,

"Men, we might be in front, but you never know what those
Cumberland players have up their sleeves."

And the first thing that goes through my mind is
they don't have footballs up their sleeves. The second thing
is, sometimes my life seems like the game between Georgia Tech
and Cumberland College. I am Cumberland College.

First the opening kickoff. Then my parakeet, Joey,
dies (FADE IN: Joey, recumbent in his cage)
before I walk into a rickety classroom
in the oldest high school west of the Appalachians.
(FADE IN: rickety classroom)

Only now the game slows down,
because, by God, I made it into college,
but Olive Littlejohn was right in the sense
I'm in over my head, and these four years—
no, let's be honest, five—seem like fifty
before the game gathers speed and, from the stands,

one by one, my grandparents, father, mother,
six aunts, and seven uncles disappear.
(FADE IN: empty stands)
"Show them no mercy!" Coach Heisman shouts.

Final score: Georgia Tech 222, Cumberland College 0

Boonesborough, Kentucky—Circa 1775

Chopping wood beside the smokehouse,
Daniel Boone explains to his hound, Simon,
"I wouldn't give a tinker's damn for a man
who isn't sometimes afraid. Fear's the spice
that makes it interesting to go ahead!"

(CUE: Simon snoring)

Evansville, Indiana—July 4, 2017

"*Mark,* you have to *do* something!" says DeeGee
while cradling Sophie, who is trembling
like a Cumberland College halfback between us on our couch
as Zach-the-ER-Doc drums up business
by lighting up his yard with an arsenal of fireworks
in proximity to neighborhood children and our house.

"She can't take this at her age," says DeeGee,
tightening the Velcro on Sophie's Thundersuit.
"It's almost ten o'clock. Please, tell Zach to *stop!*"

(Why, you might ask, is Zach-the-ER-Doc
portrayed alternately by Steve Nash, the great
NBA point guard, and Emily Dickinson?

Answer:
the unusual width between eyes—a feature contributive
to seeing an enemy point guard in the wings,
disparate elements of existence as one,
and an adrenalin-charged neighbor at ground level
while admiring a sparkle-dripping, screaming rocket overhead.)

"Hey, Dude!" Zach screams.

"Don't you know you're two days late!" I shout,
focusing on the bridge of Zach's nose.
"Just one more Newton's Nightmare," Zach pleads.

Evansville, Indiana—Fall 2009

All these years, I'd been under the impression
that people lived in houses, that people needed someone
to show them the house in which to live. Where
did Beth Ann think her imports (exports?) landed?
Yet apparently, I'd done nothing: no doctorates of anything,
not one novel written, or a single species saved.

"We have three dogs and six cats!" I tell Beth Ann.

"It was good to see you, too," Beth Ann replies.

Evansville, Indiana—July 4, 2017

While retracing my steps across the backyard,
a single   *BOOOM!*
punctuates the misinformed anniversary Festival.
"Newton's Nightmare," I whisper to myself. But then,
aside from some lame explosions a few streets over,
our block de-escalates to relative silence.

"You did it!" DeeGee exclaims. "What did you say?"
she asks as I regain my seat on the couch.

"I told Zach he'd better knock it off
if he knows what's good for him."

"I bet you did," smiling, DeeGee says,
loosening the Velcro on Sophie's Thundersuit.

THE END

3

Blue Parakeets

It's the first day of whatever month, and my shirt-tail cousin Jim
hasn't received rent for the preceding month
on a two-story duplex he owns. Jim waits until dusk,
pulls into the drive, knocks on the door.
Hard enough for it to open a smidgen.
Someone's cooking, Jim thinks. *Onions?*

"Larry!" Jim calls.

*

"I figured I owned the place, why shouldn't I go in?"
Jim told me over coffee. "Besides,
the guy owed me twelve hundred bucks."

The thing about Jim's story (aside from what's about to happen),
is that it popped into my mind out of nowhere. Actually,
in my kitchen. I was doing dishes. True,
Jim stepped into Larry's kitchen, where
a smelly stir-fry was simmering on the stove
and an empty Lone Star longneck was standing on the counter,
but it wasn't until Jim was halfway up the stairs
that his story entered my mind. I was washing a fork.
Scraping cheese from a fork.
Feta.

Why would this story—as opposed to, say, the story
of the time the great Skeeter Davis wrapped up her classic,
"Don't They Know It's the End of the World,"
by asking me, sprawled barefoot on the front row,
"Comfortable, are ya?"—come into my mind
while scraping feta from a fork?

                        Why not the moment,
forty-six years ago, when the woman I'd been seeing
told me she was engaged to an FBI agent. "But don't worry,"
she said, "he won't be back in town until next week."

Or the time I dropped a fork down the disposal.

It's like this. You've finished drying dishes.
You're putting them away: plates atop plates,
bowls within bowls. Soup spoons spooning soup spoons.
And just as you're adding a fork to its family,
a blue parakeet flies out of the drawer.
A parakeet you had when you were five.

His name was Joey.

                     *

A good rule might be:

   Don't enter another person's bedroom unless invited.

Jim's about to ignore that rule.

                     *

Not long before my great-aunt Pauline's world ended,
I visited her at The Protestant Home. A widow
after Uncle Mac died sometime in the 1950s,
Aunt Pauline was in her nineties now.
A lifetime of stories in her drawer, so to speak.

Aunt Pauline once attended the Kentucky Derby
with one of President Eisenhower's three brothers—
Milton, Earl, or Edgar. Don't ask me.
He placed a bet on every horse to win.

He won.

Once, she drove through a car wash
while wearing her mink stole.
Windows down.

"How are you today?" I asked Aunt Pauline,
taking a seat beside her bed. Looking up at me,
her blue-green eyes magnified behind thick glasses
like two earths seen from space, she said,
"I'm fine. I woke up thinking about Mac,
so I spent the morning with him.
We took a walk on a beach in Cuba."

*

But for now, Jim's ignored the rule.
He's entering the bedroom, looking around,
taking in the mess, when he smells smoke.
Turning to the closet door, he *sees* smoke,
drifting out the louvers.

Thank you for flying out, shirt-tail cousin Jim's story.
Spread your wings anytime, Skeeter, Joey. Even you,
a woman involved with a G-man. God knows
my drawer is always open for you, Aunt Pauline.

But in this case, a closet door is opening.
And if you think Larry's *bedroom* is messy,
get a load of his closet. Amidst a confusion
of shoes and a riot of clothes, Larry,
longneck in hand, cigarette in lips, says,
                                        "Hey, Jim.
I wasn't expecting you."

The Hokey Pokey

My doctor has jumped ship, going into private practice.
Very private, since I don't know where he's going.
"My blood pressure's up," I tell Christi, the sixteen-
year-old nurse practitioner assigned to me.
"Can you call in a new prescription and order bloodwork?
Oh, and don't forget to test my PSI, please."
Christi looks at me, shirtless on the table, and says,
"You mean your PS*A*, prostate-specific antigen."
Above her mask, green eyes smile.

PSI is the reading you get at the Marathon station air pump.
But considering the tire I've added to my middle,
Christi should probably order a PSI test, too. As for the questions
I had to answer on the tablet when I checked in,
*Do you feel depressed? Have you recently experienced
any feelings of hopelessness? Do you have trouble sleeping?*
Give me a break. Who doesn't? Who hasn't?
And when was the last time you slept eight hours?
No . . . no . . . no, I answered.

By now, we've reached the part of the poem
where you're expecting the bright red cardinal
that perches in a leafless tree on a bleak winter day
to shake me off the barren branch on which I've landed.
But I'm sorry, he doesn't shake me off my branch.
I'm more likely to mention the opossum couple,
Harry and Harriet, who munch on fallen seeds
each night beneath our bird feeders. One night
my wife and I were watching Harry and Harriet when,
given how Harry seems to largely ignore Harriet,
I questioned his—spell along with me now—
l-i-b-i-d-o, only I pronounced it "**li**-bido,"

accent on the li, short i, instead of li-**BEE**do. Well,
I wish you could have been there. If DeeGee's PSI
had read thirty-two pounds per square inch before I said **li**-bido,
it would have read fifteen by the time she finished laughing.
If she had had a tire pressure monitoring system,
her light would have been flashing.

In truth, I laughed, too. There we were, the two of us
shaking with laughter, frightening a cat from the room.
But when I finished laughing, I felt good. Very good.
Nothing wrong with *my* **li**-bido.

In conclusion, when you put your right foot in—
your mouth, in this instance—shake it all about.
Turn yourself around. Then (what are you waiting for?)
put your whole self in. And when you do,
notice all the people with their whole selves in,
turning themselves around, shaking all about.

That's what it's all about.

The New Yorker Cartoon Caption Contest

*It is better to write of laughter than of tears,
for laughter is the property of man.*
—François Rabelais

Monday

I'm stumped. A man angel with a giant halo
is talking to a woman angel with an average halo.
They appear to be a few feet apart,
but since they're standing in the clouds,
they could be miles apart, in which case
they are giant angels, and the man giant angel
has a *ginormous* halo, and the woman giant angel
only has a giant halo. Either way,
I have no idea what the man angel is saying,
but I have six-and-a-half days to figure it out.

Possibly, cartoonist Will McPhail had an idea
when he drew the angels for this week's contest: #526.
Or maybe he was Sullivan in search of a Gilbert.
I thought I was a Gilbert when in response to #520,
Corey Pandolph's drawing of a banana peel
slumped on a psychiatrist's couch,
I had the psychiatrist saying,

> *Depression, heart palpitations, fatigue?
> You could be low in potassium.*

Still, you have to hand it to first place winner, Michelle Deschenes
of Fort Collins, Colorado, who wrote,

> *It's normal to feel empty after a split.*

Tuesday

He never used one word when ten would do . . .

is what I'd write if someone were to draw my tombstone.
I can see why everyone might think
the angels got me thinking about my tombstone,
but I've been thinking about my tombstone
ever since the banana peel in #520 when,
before I came up with

Depression, heart palpitations, fatigue?
You could be low in potassium,

I was trying to tell the story—in two hundred fifty
characters or less—of British daredevil Bobby Leach, who,
fifteen years after going over Niagara Falls in a barrel
(breaking both knee caps and fracturing his jaw),
slipped on a banana peel in New Zealand and died,
causing the guilt-ridden peel to seek counseling.

But not only could I *not* put the Bobby Leach-
depressed-banana-peel story into so few words
(which, by now, should surprise no one),
I learned, after further research,
Bobby Leach had slipped on an *orange* peel—
which would require even more words. Nevertheless,
though forced to go with

Depression, heart palpitations, fatigue? et cetera,

I've been thinking about Bobby Leach ever since—
in the sense of tombstones and, more specifically,
you never know what's going to get you.

Or when.

Five days to go.

Wednesday

If in 1854, thirteen-year-old William Snyder had known
he would die by clown-swinging-him-around-by-the-heels,
he would have never gone to the circus, surely. On the other hand,
Greek tragedian, Aeschylus, *did know*—according to prophecy—
that he would die by a falling object. Tragically, he stayed outside,
only to have an eagle drop a tortoise on his bald head
when the eagle mistook him for a rock.

For the life of me, I can't work *guardian, snow,*
or even *angel food cake* into a caption. Four-and-a-half
days to go, and the best I've come up with
is something about the order of Angels—
like she's a lowly Principality or Power and he,
with his super-sized halo is a decorated Seraphim saying,

> *You're late for inspection, Principality!*

I wish Will McPhail had drawn an airplane
nosing through the clouds with people
staring wide-eyed out the windows at the angels
as the man angel says,

> *Ladies and gentlemen, you have just been cleared for landing.*

Thursday

In 285 BC, the poet, Philitas of Cos,
wasted away from intense study of *word usage!*
This would be about the last way I'd expect to go,

but then I doubt that twenty-one Bostonians
and three horses expected to drown in 1919
when a molasses tank burst at the Purity Distilling Company,
sending a twenty-five-feet high, thirty-five mile per hour
wave of molasses pouring through the streets of Cambridge.

The *last* way I'd expect to go is to die from uncontainable joy
when—between now and midnight, Sunday—contest editor,
Bob Mankoff changes the two hundred fifty character maximum
to an unlimited number of characters, and this poem,
"The New Yorker Cartoon Caption Contest,"
                                        WINS!

Friday

My mother's maiden name was Angel. Martha Jeanne Angel.
"I was an Angel before I met your dad," my mother,
divorced after forty-four years of marriage, liked to say.

Now my mother and my dad are angels.
The cartoon angels could be them!

   I see he's still fiddling around with words, my dad angel says.

   Not exactly wasting away, is he? asks my mother angel.
   How'd you get that great big halo, Paul?

   I've been here longer than you. It grows on you.
   But you're right, I've met Philitas of Cos.
   Our son is no Philitas of Cos.

Still, says my mother angel, *I like the poem
where we're listening to his band play "Wooly Bully,"
and the music is so loud I faint and swallow my tongue,
and you cradle my head just so and tilt my jaws
at just the right angle and plead with me
in words that only we can understand.
The poem where we still loved each other.*

Oh, Jeanne, it's normal to feel empty after a split.

Very funny, says my mother angel.

I'm sorry, my dad angel says.
Would you like to share some cake?

Saturday

My dad would have loved the story of Saint Lawrence,
patron saint of chefs, firefighters, and comedians, who,
after suffering the agony of a bed of burning coals, said,

Turn me over. I'm done on this side.

I think Saint Lawrence had the right idea,
and *The New Yorker* Cartoon Caption Contest does, too—
that as you look at the big picture, if possible, laugh

almost as hard as the seventeenth-century Scottish writer
and Rabelaisian translator, Thomas Urquhart,
who died from a fit of laughter after hearing Charles II
had been restored to the throne.

I guess you had to be there.

Sunday

12:10 AM

Given the life expectancy of the average U.S. male,
my current age *is* to the time I have remaining
to achieve lasting fame, discover the meaning of life,
and enter approximately six hundred nineteen
more cartoon caption contests

AS

12:10 Sunday morning is to the time I have left
to come up with this week's entry.

Put another way:

$$\frac{65}{76.9} = \frac{12:10 \text{ AM}}{11:59 \text{ PM}}$$

I'm inclined to go with the guy angel saying,

Hey! You! Get off of my cloud!

or maybe a simple greeting like,

Halo.

And the woman angel,
getting a good look at the man angel
with the giant if not ginormous nimbus, says,

Well, HA-LO!

My Forest Fire

My God! I think to myself, driving, eyes on Smokey,
looking down at me from a billboard—shovel in claw.
Nine out of ten humans cause forest fires? No way!
I doubt nine out of ten humans have been in a forest,

let alone set one on fire, I reason, passing Batteries + Bulbs,
The Wine Vault, and Panera while considering (and remember,
this is going through my mind as *fast* as a forest fire; plus,
I'm driving) all the times I went camping and made campfires

before slipping into my bag for the night, and how the next day
there would be a few dying embers in the pit, but it was getting late
and if I wanted to reach Lake Unforgettable or summit
Mount Not-That-Difficult by noon, I'd better get going,

so it's possible the wind kicked up after I *got* going
and sparked a spark or awakened an ember, however that works,
blowing either spark or ember onto pine needle or wood chip.
But since I preferred point-to-point hikes to out-and-back or loop

hikes, I could have missed seeing *my* forest fire altogether.
If there's one thing I know, I'm no different from everyone else.
If I'm wrong and nine out of ten of us have been in a forest,
it's possible the other eight of you have caused a fire, too.

By this time, I'm past Best Buy, approaching Logan's Road House
when I realize what all of you knew by Batteries + Bulbs,
that what Smokey really said was, "Nine out of ten forest fires
are caused by . . ." Oh, you know.

Stopped at Starbucks, streetlight as red as an ember in a fire pit,
I think that, more accurately, nine out of ten humans
have caused something *like* a forest fire. You know
how sometimes when you're in the middle of a dream

and you feel as though (and if I'm not like everyone else,
this could be embarrassing) you've killed someone,
robbed a 7-Eleven, or run over Mr. Sparkles?
So you decide to wake up, but when you do

you still feel like you've killed, robbed, or run over,
and the feeling sticks with you through breakfast
until finally, you think the someone, 7-Eleven, or Mr. Sparkles
is a stand-in for some terrible thing you've *really* done

or a not-so-terrible thing that resulted in a terrible thing,
and since life is point-to-point and not out-and-back or a
loop, you might not know what either the not-so-terrible thing
you did or the terrible thing you caused was. Imagine

you're a cow walking out of a shed at 137 DeKoven Street
in Chicago, Illinois, on October 8, 1871. You're munching hay,
flicking your tail, thinking how it wouldn't hurt Mrs. O to use
a little lotion on her hands, and also, *Holy cow, this hay is dry!*

completely unaware, you just flicked over the lantern
that will result in the deaths of 300 people, the destruction
of 3.3 square miles, and leave 100,000 homeless. By now
I'm turning into my drive, waving at my neighbor, Joe.

If ever someone has just remembered a not-so-terrible thing
that sparked a terrible thing, Joe could be the guy,
listlessly raking leaves in his front yard. But wait. If my
nine-out-of-ten-not-so-terrible-thing causation premise is correct,

isn't it possible that nine out of ten of us (Joe included) have done a fairly-good thing that caused a good or possibly *great* thing? Wouldn't Joe want to know? "Hey, Joe!" I shout.
But Joe just looks at me, drops his rake, and runs into his house.

Carrying On

Rejoice, rejoice, we have no choice but to carry on.
　—Crosby, Stills, Nash, and Young, "Carry On"

1.

May 14, 1:25 AM.

Awakened by throbs of throbbing bass, car
doors slamming, and rapid-fire bursts
of shouts and laughter, we leap from bed,
DeeGee out one side, me, the other,
meeting at the foot and following the sounds into my office,
where I crack the blinds and see a gang of hoodlums in our yard!

"Where's the phone?" I ask.
"Turn on a light!" I shout. "My glasses!"

　　　　　　　　　*

On a typical, sleep-filled night, if our bed were a map
of Illinois, Indiana, Kentucky, and much of Ohio,
I'd be Illinois and DeeGee, Indiana. One dog, Scout,
fills greater Chicago. Chica stretches across Kentucky.
Mr. Peabody snoozes from Columbus to Cleveland.
Oddly, throughout the ruckus, they lie undisturbed.

　　　　　　　　　　　　　Some watchdogs,
I think as more automobiles turn onto our street. "Operator,
I'm calling from 1124 Glenmoor Court (as if she doesn't know).
There must be twenty cars outside our house!
There must be fifty people in the street and in our yard!
They're out there carrying on!"

                              Is it just me,
or does everyone seem as though they're in their twenties?
My doctor wears sneakers. My plumber has an ear disc.

"What are they carrying *on*, sir?" the operator asks
as though a 747 were boarding in our driveway.
"No, they're *carrying* on," I make clear. And then
there's a pause on her end—long enough
for her to ask an older, wiser supervisor
what *carrying on* means—before she, the youngster,
comes back on the line and says,
"It's probably an after-graduation party, sir."

                                        In this moment,
recalling sad, horn music wafting from the direction
of a nearby high school earlier that night,
I remember that our neighbors Harold and Carol's
six-year-old son, Ethan, a Cub Scout who sold stale popcorn
(what? two, three years ago?), could be eighteen. "Oh,"
I say as DeeGee slides my glasses onto my face
and the happy grads streaming through our yard come into focus.

"An officer is on the way," the operator says.

"No, wait, it's all right. It's only Eth—"
                                        But she is gone.

2.

Sometimes I feel like an okapi: endangered cousin to the giraffe.
Zebralike, chocolate-colored stripes on my four legs;

an eighteen-inch-long, purplish-black, prehensile tongue
to clean my giant rotating ears; and eyeballs that retract
in eyeball-threatening, northeast Congolese rainforests.

"She's never heard of carrying on," I say, settling into Illinois.

"At least you said cars instead of automobiles," says DeeGee,
back home again in Indiana.

I could remind DeeGee how she calls our bisque
Whirlpool side-by-side an icebox
in addition to the wooden, antique icebox
that serves as a pantry in our kitchen—
problematic when I want to find the Newman's Own
Medium Black Bean and Corn Salsa, say, as in:

"Where's the Newman's?"

"It's in the icebox."

Instead, I go with, "What's wrong with *automobile?*"

"No one says it anymore but you."

"At least I didn't say *ruckus*."

*

Imagine the Wabash River rippling with laughter
as it flows between Illinois and Indiana into The Ohio.
So we're laughing at my "carrying on" and "ruckus."
You might even say we're *carrying on* at my "carrying on"

and "ruckus"—and *carrying* even more *on* when I say,

"Hoodlums,"

and DeeGee replies with:

"Hoodlums in their autoMObiles"
(as if I pronounce automobile, *autoMObile*).

"At least she called me sir instead of sweetie," I say,
as a flashing light revolves around our bedroom.

The police autoMObile has arrived.

3.

Interestingly, *ruckus* is a circa 1890 Americanism
of the words *ruction* (meaning "disturbance")
and *rumpus* (meaning "uproar").

At least I didn't say ruction.
At least I didn't say rumpus.

My sweet grandmother Elsie Angel was born in 1891.
To think that Grandma Angel grew up with words like
razzmatazz, chew the fat, hooligan, and *ruckus,*
not that long after *automobile* and *hoodlum*.
To think that words, like people, come into the world and leave it,
words like *spermologer, snoutfair, jirble,* and *kench,*
and people like Grandma Angel, DeeGee, and me.

4.

But in the meantime, car doors are slamming, minus
the rapid-fire bursts of shouts and laughter
(the officer, no doubt, quashing the ruckus),
when I turn to DeeGee and say,
"Have I ever told you about the time—"
                                        "Yes."
"Well," I say, "when I was fourteen . . ."

Once again, I describe the night my friend Curt and I
decided it would be a good idea to take off all our clothes
and race a lap around Saint Michael's Episcopal Church.
But just as we rounded the building, a Corvette rounded the corner.
"It's Darleen Hart and her boyfriend!" Curt yelled.

Deserting Curt, I zipped into the Sheehan's backyard,
a yard I had mowed earlier that week
when there was no badminton net in place—
a badminton net that caught me in the face
and flung me to my back onto the wet Bermuda.

"Then a light came on," I tell DeeGee,
"a window opened, and Doctor Sheehan yelled,
"What's all the ruckus!"

"He didn't say that last time," laughs DeeGee.
And then we carry on some more.

5.

Snoutfair: someone with a handsome face, as in:
The okapi is no snoutfair.

Kench: to laugh loudly, as in:
The operator kenched when she hung up the phone.

Spermologer: one who picks up trivia, as in:
Sometimes the old spermologer feels like an okapi.

Jirble: to pour out a liquid with an unsteady hand, as in:
I'm sorry I jirbled your coffee, sweetie.

6.

Ruckus quashed, doorbell ringing; Chica,
Scout, and Mr. Peabody jump from bed and bark.
Now *they're* carrying on as I follow them down the hall—
a blue bathrobe covering my chocolate stripes,
my eyeballs protruding.

Usually, the only thing that stops our dogs from barking
is a spritz from a squirt bottle that we keep by our front door.
Two o'clock in the morning, I'm spritzing,
and one by one the dogs quit barking.
"That won't be necessary, sir," a twenty-fiveish-
year-old police officer says as I open the storm door
and realize my bottle's aimed at him.
"It's only water," I explain, lowering my bottle.
"I'm sorry I ruined Ethan's party."
                              "Don't be," he says.
"The party went viral on Twitter. His mother said to say thanks."

7.

May 14, 2:10 AM

"The party went viral on Twitter. Carol said to say thanks,"
I tell DeeGee as the dogs and I return to bed
and Indiana fills with laughter.

"What's so funny about that?" I ask.

"It just doesn't sound like you—*viral on Twitter.*"

We kench ourselves to sleep.

Heaven's Rules

Sometimes, I imagine my mother and dad
sitting around a Heavenly table with their friends,
some old—*Hi, Ruth. Hi, Walt*—some new. No
cards. No board games. No scoresheet.
But every so often, one of them smiles,
licks a finger, and makes a mark in the air.
First to ten wins.

My dad never shied away from competition.
Mother counted Christmas cards each year. So,
I thought I'd help them out, put smiles on their faces,
marks in the air, by thinking about them
and telling you this:

It's 1960-something. My dad is in our dining room
with one of those pump-action sprayers
and a bucket of water. He's wetting down
flowery wallpaper before stripping it. Meanwhile,
one wall away in our pink bathroom, my mother
is taking a bubble bath. Dad is spraying,
Mother is bubbling when Dad gets an idea.
Knocking on the bathroom door, sprayer in hand, he shouts,
"Jeanne, I'm about to burst!
Pull the curtains. I'm coming in."

By Heaven's rules, before starting a new game,
each player has to scoop their points from the air
and offer them to someone who hasn't been thought of in a while,
like Mohammad Arif, an Iraqi sheepherder who died in 1653
and was last remembered in 1697 by his grandson Baba,
who told the story of Mohammad driving off a pack of jackals
with Great-grandfather Jafar's crook.

Or Constance Stillwater, a Cherokee teen
who died on the Trail of Tears
and hasn't been thought of since 1889.

Why would points mean anything to someone
who hasn't scored them, you might ask.
But think about it, you can't very well give your points
to someone without thinking about them, can you?
And to quote Christian mystic philosopher/theologian
Emanuel Swedenborg, *All in Heaven take joy in sharing
their delights and blessings with others.*
(One point to Swedenborg.)

By now, Dad is in the bathroom. And though
you're probably way ahead of me on this,
he's pumping water from the pink toilet
and spraying it back in, while audibly sighing.
For minutes on end, pumping . . . sighing . . .
until my mother, grown increasingly silent,
shouts from behind the curtain,
"My gosh, Paul!"

And lest you think my parents
might be embarrassed by this low drama, know
that another one of Heaven's rules is:
NO EMBARRASSMENT ALLOWED. Likewise
GUILT, ANGER, SHAME, et cetera. Also,
LAUGHTER GREATLY ENCOURAGED,
the kind of laughter my mother and father shared
each time the wallpaper-stripping story was told.

This time, my mother is first to ten.
A Heavenly trumpet blows *RHA-RHA,* and Mother
scoops her points and offers them to Mohammed.

My mother used to offer chocolate candy (the good stuff:
Hershey Nuggets Special Dark with Almonds, Werther's
Original Caramel Chocolate Dark, and Rollo
Chewy Caramels in Milk Chocolate)
to every waiter and waitress who served her,
and when they accepted—as Mohammed
accepts Mother's points now—
their smile made Mother smile, too.

Dad hands his points to Constance Stillwater,
and Ruth and Walt give theirs to Zhang Wei,
a fourteenth-century Buddhist priest,
and Shomari Abimbola, a Bantu healer, respectively.
Then Mother, Dad, Ruth, and Walt
float back to the table and start a new game.

Autobituary

June 26, 2046, *Evansville Courier & Press*

I, Mark Williams, a resident of Evansville, Indiana, died
of expected causes on my 95th birthday, June 24, 2046.
Hoping to enter Heaven, Paradise, Moksha, or Nirvana—
Sanskrit for *blown out*—that very day, I wrote this years before.

Life is good, at least for me. And hopefully,
by putting this into the cosmos, my chances
of reaching ninety-five will be increased because,
for all anyone knows, it works that way. But also,
after considering my grandma Mabel's lament to my dad,
"Oh, Paul, I feel like I'm a hundred years old"
and my dad's reply, "Well, Mother, you are ninety-eight,"
ninety-five is plenty, for as Mark Twain wrote,
*Lord, save us from old age, broken health, and a hope tree
that has lost its faculty of putting out blossoms.* So,
by putting this into the cosmos, I'll blow out at ninety-five.
Since it might work that way, too. But in case THE DAY arrives,
I don't blow out, and my hope tree is still blossoming,
I'll be so afraid of dying that day, I'll die that day
and remove the certainty of becoming
a hope tree that can no longer blossom. Like being
on a low-carb diet and going to Starbucks with The Cosmos
and saying, "Don't let me get the Iced Lemon Pound Cake."
But when The Cosmos turns its big head, I order it anyway,
only to have The Cosmos yank it from my hands.

Still, after comparing life past ninety-five to a piece of cake,
I thought about trashing this. To Hell, The Bardo,
The Chinvat Bridge, or Samsara with the carbs.
But by then, this was in the cosmos.
There was nothing I could do.
Memorial service to be held at any time
with anyone at the Starbucks nearest you.

About the Author

Mark Williams is retired from the real estate business in Evansville, Indiana. His poems have found homes in *The Hudson Review, The Southern Review, Able Muse, Rattle*, *Nimrod, New Ohio Review, The American Journal of Poetry,* and the anthologies, *New Poetry from the Midwest* (New American Press) and *The Sixty-Four: Best Poets of 2018* (The Black Mountain Press). His long poem, "Happiness," was published as a chapbook by Finishing Line Press in 2015. His fiction has appeared or is forthcoming in *Indiana Review, The Nonconformist, Drunk Monkeys, fresh.ink, The Peauxdunque Review, SPLASH!,* and the anthologies, *American Fiction* (New Rivers Press), *The Boom Project: Voices of a Generation* (Butler Books), *Running Wild Novella Anthology, Volume 4,* and *Running Wild Anthology of Stories, Volume 5* (Running Wild Press).

www.ingramcontent.com/pod-product-compliance
Lightning Source LLC
Chambersburg PA
CBHW031200160426
43193CB00008B/454